COUNTDOWN

>>> TO THE <<<

SECOND COMING

a chronology

of

prophetic events

happening

now

DAVE HUNT

BEND • OREGON

Except where otherwise indicated, all Scripture quotations in this book are taken from the King James Version of the Bible.

COUNTDOWN TO THE SECOND COMING

Copyright © 2014
Published by The Berean Call
PO Box 7019, Bend, OR 97708-7020

ISBN: 978-1-928660-19-4
Large Print ISBN: 978-1-68138-004-9
Giant Print ISBN: 978-1-68138-005-6

Previously published in hardcover under ISBN: 1-928660-10-X

PRINTED IN THE UNITED STATES OF AMERICA

Contents

1
THE ULTIMATE FALSEHOOD >>> 5

2
PEACEFUL WORDS, PROVOCATIVE DEEDS >>> 15

3
ARE WE THERE YET? >>> 27

4
MEASURING WHAT CANNOT BE MEASURED >>> 43

5
INFINITE MYSTERY, PERPETUAL JOY >>> 69

6
THE ULTIMATE HOPE >>> 79

ENDNOTES >>> 94

Little children, it is the last time: and as ye have heard that antichrist shall come, even now are there many antichrists; whereby we know that it is the last time.

—1 John 2:18

< 1 >

The Ultimate Falsehood

SOMEWHERE AT THIS VERY MOMENT on Planet Earth, the Antichrist is almost certainly alive—biding his time, awaiting his cue. Banal sensationalism? Far from it! That likelihood is based upon a sober evaluation of current events in relation to Bible prophecy. Already a mature man, the Antichrist is perhaps active in politics and might even be an admired world leader. Or he could be the head of a multinational corporation, a little-known international banker of great wealth and behind-the-scenes influence, a sports hero—or he might arise suddenly from total anonymity. Somewhere he is being meticulously groomed, though as yet he probably has no more inkling

< 5 >

than do those who encounter him daily of the ultimate role for which Satan is preparing him and will, one momentous day, utterly possess him.

Whoever and wherever he is, one passion rules this remarkable man—a lust for power. Even so, benevolence, prudence, integrity, and principle mark his circumspect public behavior. It may be that at this point in his life he is still convinced that his motives are altogether pure and unselfish.

Antichrist! The media has so conditioned our minds that the very word instantly conjures up the image of a sinister man who exudes evil from every pore. But Hollywood caricatures play into the hands of the real Antichrist, since no suspicion will rest upon this one whose admirable qualities so well conceal his dark designs. When the time has come for his surprising world takeover, precipitated by an unprecedented global crisis, he will be hailed as the world's savior, and so he will appear to be.

The Apostle Paul dispels popular misconceptions and gives us the awesome facts: "Satan himself is transformed into an angel of light. Therefore it is no great thing if his ministers also be transformed as the ministers of righteousness..." (2 Corinthians 11:14,15). We may be certain that Antichrist will appear as the purest "angel of light" that Satan can produce.

Society has been undergoing a step-by-step preparation for the advent of Satan's messiah, and in our moment of history has at last produced a generation so perverted that it will actually mistake the Antichrist for Christ. In the name of freedom and right of choice, our most blessed of nations has condemned its unborn to the cruelest of deaths, has made a mockery of the sanctity of marriage, entertains itself with films and music centered on themes of violence, Satanism, and sexual perversions, has all but destroyed millions of its youth with drugs, and has created an urban war zone and a poisoned planet. Evil will soon be ripe for harvest.

Jesus warned that *many* would come claiming to be the Christ. These numerous lesser antichrists who were already in the world, as the apostle John explained in 1 John 2:18, would prepare the way for the real Antichrist who would appear in the last of the "last days." Behold the ultimate deception: Satan posing as God, Antichrist masquerading as the true Christ, and not just the world, but an apostate church as well, totally taken in by the bold fraud. Instead of a frontal assault on Christianity, the evil one will pervert the church *from within* by posing as its founder. He will cunningly misrepresent Christ while pretending to *be* Christ. And by that process of substitution, he will undermine and pervert all that Christ truly is. Anything less than such a diabolically malevolent strategy would be unworthy of Satan's foul genius.

This is an altogether different scenario from that envisioned by most people. If they believe in a literal Antichrist at all, they presume he will be an obviously evil ogre whom any child would immediately recognize. In fact, however, he will be the closest counterfeit of Christ that Satan can produce. Completely deceived by this brazen masquerade, the world will hail him as its deliverer.

And right there is where the plot thickens. If the Antichrist will indeed pretend to be the Christ, then his followers must be "Christians"! The church of that day will, with scarcely a dissenting voice, hail him as its leader.

Such perversion and deception are beyond the ability of the imagination to conceive. It is certainly not what the average person has been led to believe. Yet this is the picture which the Bible presents and to which current events ever more clearly seem to point.

How Could This Be?

It becomes immediately apparent that such an unthinkable scenario requires certain preconditions to make it credible. First of all, the apostate church in the last days must become so corrupted that it actually opposes what Christ taught, while at the same time insisting that it is faithful to Him. Satan's lie will be honored as God's truth without the church leaders who deceive, and those who are deceived, even knowing that such a metamorphosis has taken place. Moreover, the preparation for the great delusion must have been well in process from within the "last days" church itself even before the Antichrist appears.

Could Paul have meant anything less when he warned, "Let no man deceive you by any means: for that day shall not come, except there come a falling away [apostasy, turning from the faith] first, and [then] that man of sin [the Antichrist] be revealed, the son of perdition" (2 Thessalonians 2:3)? In that day, sound doctrine will be despised (2 Timothy 4:1-4). For many people, objective truth will have been replaced by feelings and experience. For others, intellectualism and skepticism will have justified what will seem to be a very reasonable improvement upon "Christianity."

Jesus himself, who raised the question whether there would be any faith whatsoever on the earth when He returned (Luke 18:8), used language similar to Paul's. When His disciples asked Him what would characterize the last days just prior to His return, Jesus explained that it would be a time of the greatest religious deception the world had seen to that point, or would ever see again. He prefaced His remarks with this solemn warning: "Take heed that no man *deceive you*" (Matthew 24:4; cf. 5,11,24).

Those who truly know the Lord and heed such warnings will not succumb to the spirit of the last days. Like God, who weeps over a rebellious world and delays His judgment to give men time to repent, they will have a passion to bring His truth to the world. Everyone who loves God more than this world, and to whom His evaluation of one's life means more than the fickle opinions of men, will be kept from the delusion that will sweep the world. Those who fear God and keep His Word have no fear of what others may think or say or do to them, because they fear God with deep reverence.

Preparation for Delusion

The world must be prepared both religiously and politically to embrace the Antichrist when he suddenly rises to power. If "Christianity" is to be the official world religion (which must be the case if the Antichrist claims to be Christ returned), then it must become broad enough to accommodate all of the world's faiths. As for the political climate, the world must be united in the twin causes of global peace and ecological rescue when this man appears.

Through the many astonishing events of recent years, political leaders have found themselves suddenly and almost miraculously transported into a new world where worldwide peace and unity seem within reach. For decades, Westerners lived in fear lest communist totalitarianism move west to swallow the free world. But suddenly, before our very eyes we see a surprising new picture emerging, taking even the most brilliant strategists completely by surprise: Democracy is moving east! The united response to terrorism is forging a new world. At the same time, the competition for a share of the exploding world market is forcing change upon even communist nations.

China has suppressed those seeking democratic reforms,

yet even she must eventually succumb to world opinion or suffer increasingly costly isolation from an emerging and growing international community, which has become remarkably united commercially. The Islamic world, too, remains tied to its own agenda and is still susceptible to the sudden call for a "Holy War" against the rest of mankind. But in Arab countries as well as the rest of the world there is a fermenting opposition to autocratic rulers, both religious and secular, and a great longing for democracy that cannot be denied much longer. The native dictatorships in Africa have proven to be worse than the overthrown colonialism, and it may be only a matter of time until these and fundamental Islamic movements are pushed out by popular uprisings. The expulsion of Charles Taylor from Liberia; the death by cancer of the former murderous dictator of Uganda, Idi Amin; the ousting and death of murderer and embezzler of billions, Nigeria's former military dictator General Sani Abacha; and the ouster of Indonesia's ruthless and corrupt General Suharto (and others suffering similar fates) may be encouraging indicators of how autocratic third-world rulers (Zimbabwe's Mugabe et al.) and regimes will fare in the near future.

Within a surprisingly short time, it may actually seem that mankind has at last, in the name of freedom, united to eliminate the threat of major war from this planet. Global peace will have been achieved at last. Strangely enough, that may be the worst thing that could happen, as we shall see.

In the following pages, we will trace events and processes that appear to be putting the props and players in place for Antichrist's grand entry onto center stage. The curtain is soon to rise upon the final act of human history as we have known it. Although God has deliberately hidden much from our eyes, He has told us what He wants us to know about the incredible face-to-face confrontation between Christ and Antichrist toward which events now hasten—and concerning the part that each of us must play.

Prophecy is a difficult subject, and many people have been disillusioned by conflicting and often sensational interpretations. Others feel that the subject is necessarily morbid and depressing and therefore to be avoided. But the true picture is not all gloom and doom, since prophecy also offers an unprecedented opportunity for those who, understanding the "signs of the times," are willing to believe and act upon what the Bible declares for our day.

> Roman Catholic Church (Christian Church) exclusive.
> Its ministers proven to be in darkness.
> Falling away with no belief in objective truth.
> False gospel of infant baptism and sacraments.
> MisTranslation of sacraments (should be) "mystery".
   priest (should be) elder.
   penance (should be) Repentance.
> Dissent silenced.
> Political Christianity in America + Israel
> Leader Trump
> Achieving Peace in middle east 2020!!
> False news dominant
> Truth bastardised.
> Intellectual scepticism

And all things are of God, who hath

reconciled us to himself by Jesus Christ,

and hath given to us the ministry of

reconciliation...

—2 CORINTHIANS 5:18

< 2 >

Peaceful Words, Provocative Deeds

IN SPITE OF TERRORISM and looming war clouds in the Middle East, the prospect of a peace such as the world has never known seems to be a realistic hope. That the nations of the world will indeed establish an unprecedented international peace, and perhaps fairly soon, is certain, because the Bible has for thousands of years foretold a false peace in the last days.

That time of peace is prophesied, however, not with joy but with sorrow, for the prophets declared that it would precede a holocaust that would threaten the survival of all life on this

< 15 >

planet. Why? The answer to this question comprises the entire subject matter of the Bible, which in fact prophesies the coming of *two* periods of global peace. The first will be realized for a time under the Antichrist, and the second will be established by the return of Jesus Christ in power and glory to rule this planet where He was so cruelly rejected and crucified.

Earth's war-weary inhabitants will greet the first period of peace ecstatically, convinced that the Millennium has dawned. And, for a time, it will appear that the world's economic, social, and ecological problems have been solved. That will, however, be a great delusion. Biblical prophets have warned that this false peace will usher in the Great Tribulation (after Christ takes His church to heaven in the "Rapture") and will culminate seven years later in the most destructive war in earth's history—Armageddon! In somber revelation, the Apostle Paul declared:

> When they [the world, not true Christians] shall say, Peace and safety; then sudden destruction cometh upon them as travail upon a woman with child; and they shall not escape. (1 Thessalonians 5:3)

On the one hand, it seems incomprehensible that international peace at last attained should be the prelude to disaster. Yet what else could result from a "peace" established by Antichrist? As always, so today, the world's leaders pursue their negotiations among themselves in utter disregard for the essential role that must be played by the Prince of Peace, Jesus Christ. If mankind could by its own efforts establish a just and lasting peace, it would disprove the Bible—which declares that true peace can come only through Jesus Christ reigning upon earth. In fact, all such humanistic attempts are doomed by man's inherent sinfulness.

Where Are the Voices of True Peace?

Are we suggesting that the world's leaders shouldn't even attempt to achieve global peace? Of course, they must try. But those who are not Christians, driven by necessity to pursue every possible means to establish peace, don't realize the futility of their efforts. Christian political leaders, of course, are also compelled to join their secular colleagues in pursuing world peace. At the same time, they must declare solemnly and clearly to the rest of the world that the only true hope for global peace is to repent for having violated God's laws, to receive Jesus Christ as the Savior who has died for the sins of the world, and then to ask Him to come back to this earth to reign.

Where are the Christian political leaders with the courage to do so? And if they did, who would listen? To stand fully for Christ without any compromise would end any political leader's career.

Peter explained to the first Gentile converts after Christ's resurrection that *peace* was to be *preached* through Jesus

Christ (Acts 10:36). To most of today's Christians, that is a radical thought. What pastor or evangelist on radio or television today is preaching *global peace* through Jesus Christ? Paul declared that this peace was both "to you which were afar off [Gentiles] and to them that were near [Jews]" (Ephesians 2:17)—and that this peace was only possible through Christ having died for the sins of the world (2 Corinthians 5:18,19).

Those who set out to establish international peace through a world government over which the Lord Jesus Christ is not invited to reign are necessarily on the side of Antichrist. They are preparing the world for his rule, whether or not they recognize or acknowledge that fact. Such is the danger that attends all earthly efforts to establish international peace and unity.

The Delusion of Ecumenism

There are only two persons who will hold absolute rule over this world. The first is the Antichrist and the second is the Lord Jesus Christ. Every person must choose between these two antagonists and their opposing kingdoms. There is no neutral ground.

Those who suggest that we can retain the idea of Christ's return to reign over Planet Earth as the *symbol* of some "spiritual truth" suitable for all religions deny the very foundation of the Christian faith. Christianity is based upon the claims

that Christ made about *Himself* and the eyewitness accounts
of His life, death, and resurrection as recorded in the New
Testament in undeniable fulfillment of Old Testament prophecies. The distinctions that make Christianity unique are irrec-
oncilable with any other religious belief, and any attempt at
ecumenical unity is a denial of biblical Christianity. Consistent
with the distinctiveness of Christianity, the Bible also teaches
that peace will not come to this world through the triumph
of Christ's *teachings*, but only through His *personal return to
reign from Jerusalem.* In fact, His teachings cannot be separated from Himself. That was the very challenge with which
Jesus confronted the Jewish religious leaders in His day:

> Search the scriptures, for in them ye think ye have
> eternal life: and they are they which testify of me. And
> ye will not come to me, that ye might have life. (John
> 5:39,40)

How dare anyone think that a world ripening for judgment can be rescued by Christians working together in politi-
cal/social activism with the followers of all religions, and with
humanists and atheists! Scripture says repeatedly that nothing
but the personal and physical return of Christ to this earth can
put an end to its wickedness and suffering. Paul declared that
"the whole creation groaneth and travaileth in pain together"
as it longs for a release that can come only through "the

manifestation of the sons of God" (Romans 8:19-22). Paul makes very clear what this means: That only when Christians have received their immortal bodies and are glorified with Christ (verses 23-25), ruling and reigning upon this earth with Him, will earth be delivered from its turmoil and pain.

The last days before Christ's return are indeed prophesied as a period of growing evil, error, and spiritual delusion, manifested in both the world and the professing church. There are also, however, indications in Scripture that in the last days, millions of people around the world will receive Christ as Savior and Lord, thus hastening His return. Many of them will be the most unlikely candidates for salvation—New Agers, drug addicts, prison inmates, communists, Muslims, Catholics, the poor and the outcasts of society—as Christ seemed to indicate in the parable of the great supper:

> Then the master of the house being angry [at those who accepted his invitation, but failed to come to the feast and tried to cover up their unwillingness with pitiful excuses] said to his servant, Go out quickly into the streets and lanes of the city, and bring in hither the poor, and the maimed, and the halt, and the blind.
>
> And the servant said, Lord, it is done as thou hast commanded, and yet there is room. And the lord said unto the servant, Go out into the highways and hedges, and compel them to come in, that my house may be filled. (Luke 14:21-23)

Evangelicals tend to present the gospel exclusively as a remedy for personal sin and the procurement of an eternal home in heaven. They generally neglect to proclaim it as God's means of bringing peace to this troubled planet, as did the angels at the birth of Christ and as did the early church. It is the duty of every Christian political leader, whether president, ambassador, or other official, to make very clear to the entire world that all human efforts to achieve peace are in vain unless Jesus Christ is invited back to this earth to reign in individual hearts and over all nations.

Viewing Current Events Through Scripture

From the perspective of biblical prophecy, extreme caution is in order, rather than the popular euphoria, in appraising the recent introduction of new freedoms in communist nations and improved relations with the West. We dare not neglect the guidance of Scripture in evaluating current events. And if we will heed God's Word, we will see that what we have been witnessing increasingly around the world could well be leading not to the solution of mankind's problems but to history's greatest disaster.

How can we make such a definite declaration? Isn't it dangerous to attempt to correlate current events with biblical prophecy? Indeed it is. Nevertheless, if Bible prophecy concerning the "last days" is truly inspired of God, the time must come when what the prophets have written describes current developments.

The euphoria of millions freed from communist rule in Eastern Europe and the former Soviet Union was quickly followed by the misery of even worse poverty. Government oppression was replaced by increasing lawlessness, the influx of cults, the explosion of incipient immorality, corruption, and occultism. The Eastern republics witnessed an Islamic takeover with accompanying terrorism. Is history repeating its endless cycle? Humanistic hopes for a new and better world seemingly find justification in technology's amazing promises. Yet biblical prophecy offers sober insights to those who will give heed.

William Manchester's gripping biography of Sir Winston Churchill confronts us with unpleasant and haunting reminders of Hitler—a man who came extremely close to being the Antichrist, and who deceived the entire world for a time with his promises of peace:

> Thomas Jones, who had been in and out of Whitehall for a quarter century, wrote in his diary: "...all sorts of people who have met Hitler are convinced that he is a factor for peace...."
>
> Meeting the press after he had been closeted with Hitler for an hour, Lloyd George said he regarded him as "the greatest living German...."
>
> Arnold Toynbee...equally spellbound by the Reich chancellor, declared that he was "convinced of his

sincerity in desiring peace in Europe and close friend-
ship with England."[1]

Winston Churchill was not deceived by Hitler, but he stood
almost alone in warning the world that the Führer's real inten-
tions would envelop Europe in war. Looking back with the clear
view we now have, it seems incredible that the leading fig-
ures of the day were almost unanimous in their praise of the
irrational demigod who had become Germany's leader, and
in their confidence that peace was assured. The deception was
well-nigh universal. Yet the rising political star whom everyone praised was a dangerous megalomaniac who would one
day take his place with the most inhumane monsters in history.
Moreover, he had frankly revealed his evil designs from the
very beginning, in *Mein Kampf* and other writings, and in his
speeches. Yet so hopeful was the world for peace at any price
that almost no one was willing to face the painful truth.

So it is today. Like Churchill in England, Netanyahu is one
of the few Israeli leaders who was not deceived by Arafat's
promises at Oslo. He wrote: "…my party and I were virtually
isolated in our warning that Arafat would not keep his word….
We were widely castigated as enemies of peace…. Our argument was that handing Gaza over to Arafat would immediately
create a lush terrorist haven…." Of course, he was right.[2]

History has proven again and again that international
leaders can be both mistaken and misunderstood. Key events

can be badly misconstrued. Assurances of peace and security can seem never more certain than when the world, in fact, is teetering on the very brink of disaster. On the other hand, the worldwide terrorism still unchecked despite another Gulf War (this time with Iraq conquered) and continuing hopelessness in Israel, could very well be the necessary catalyst to bring about the prophesied false peace. The unforgettable statement by Tajikistan's ambassador to the UN at the UN's emergency session in the wake of the devastation on September 11, 2001, may well be prophetic: "Nothing else in history or even conceivable could possibly unite the world as this event."

Unfortunately, truth in politics is almost impossible to uncover—which makes it all the more important that we discern what the Bible says. If ever there were a time when we needed to ask God for wisdom and seek to understand what His Word has prophesied for our own day, it is now.

Deception.

False peace in time of crisis.

Antichrist or christs.

lone voices castigated.

Technology progress deceptive

And as he sat upon the mount of Olives, the
disciples came unto him privately, saying,
Tell us, when shall these things be? and what
shall be the sign of thy coming, and of the
end of the world?

—Matthew 24:3

< 3 >

Are We There Yet?

I WELL REMEMBER, as a youth in the late 1930s, listening with growing conviction to the many traveling preachers who visited our small fellowship of believers to present from familiar scriptures the prophesied "signs" that would herald the approach of Christ's second coming. Though not as prevalent as it is today, even at that time there was skepticism among some Christians concerning "last days" prophecy. What could be the value of speculating about future events? Why not get on with living our lives faithfully in the present and leave the

< 27 >

future to God? After all, whatever was going to happen would come to pass in its appointed time and way, so why worry about it prematurely?

There were those, however, who had implicit faith in Bible prophecy and believed that it was intended to present recognizable "signs of the times" to guide the attitudes and actions of a future generation that would be taken alive into heaven at Christ's return. Such was the view of my godly parents. I remember the lively discussions about the place current developments had in the prophetic scheme. What was the significance of the 1929 stock market crash and the Great Depression that followed it during the 1930s? Where did President Roosevelt's New Deal, with its innovative economic and banking measures, fit in?

There were several basic premises that evangelicals in those days generally considered essential to a proper interpretation of "last days" prophecies but that seem to have been largely forgotten today. First of all, one had to differentiate between the *church* and *Israel*, each of which had a unique relationship to God and Christ. Failure to discern to which of these two entities a prophecy pertained would lead to great confusion in one's understanding of "last days" events. With proper discernment, however, prophecy would shed valuable light on the present and future, while prophecies already fulfilled, when recognized as such, would provide irrefutable evidence that the Bible was God's Word.

Second, one had to distinguish between the Rapture and the *Second Coming* of Christ. These were viewed as two separate events. The Rapture would be for the church, when Christ would catch her up to meet Him in the air and take her as His bride to His Father's house of many mansions for a glorious heavenly marriage and honeymoon. The Second Coming would be for Israel seven years later, when Christ would come visibly to this earth, in power and glory *with His church,* to rescue His chosen people from the armies of the Antichrist, and to begin His thousand-year reign from David's restored throne in Jerusalem.

Distinctions that Matter

Before the cross of Christ, mankind was divided into two groups: Jews and Gentiles. Both the Old and New Testaments make very clear what caused this distinction: the everlasting covenants that God had made with Abraham, Isaac, and Jacob, and with their descendants through Moses. These covenants were *for Israel alone* and separated her from all other nations on the face of the earth (Leviticus 20:24-26; Psalm 147:2,19-20), thereby making God's "chosen people" absolutely unique.

This important distinction between Jews and Gentiles is maintained consistently throughout the Bible: "Ye [Gentiles] were without Christ, being aliens from the commonwealth of

Israel, and strangers from the covenants of promise, having no hope and without God..." (Ephesians 2:12).

After the Cross, a new entity was born: the *church* that Christ promised He would build (Matthew 16:18). As a result, there are now three divisions of mankind: *Jews*, *Gentiles*, and the *church*. Paul tells us that we are to "give none offense, neither to the Jews, nor to the Gentiles, nor to the church of God" (I Corinthians 10:32). It is essential to understand that these three distinct groups exist side by side in today's world and will continue to do so until the end of the Millennium. We must keep a clear distinction between them and recognize that God deals with each group differently. This is fundamental when it comes to interpreting prophecy.

Scripture makes it clear that the church did not replace Israel but came into existence as a new and third entity consisting of both Jews and Gentiles, and distinct from each. As surely as Gentiles continue to exist outside the church, so also does Israel, with all of God's promises and plans for her remaining in full force. In fact, most "last days" prophecies are concerned with Israel, for she will continue here upon earth to face the Antichrist and the "time of Jacob's trouble" (Jeremiah 30:7) after the church has been raptured to heaven. As for the church, God's plans for her are unique, and different from His plans for either Israel or the Gentile nations.

In summary, prophecy becomes clouded in confusion if we fail to remember that the timing, manner, and purpose of the

Lord's coming are different for "Jews, Gentiles, and the church of God." The use of vague or ambiguous terms such as "Jesus is coming again" or "the return of Christ" or "Christ is coming" can cause misunderstanding. Coming for whom? Returning for whom? Returning to do what? For the church or for Israel and the nations? As the Bridegroom to take his bride to His Father's house, or as the Lion of the tribe of Judah to destroy those who have destroyed Israel? It makes a great difference.

Consider, for example, Matthew 24:29,30: "Immediately after the tribulation...shall appear the sign of the Son of man in heaven...and they shall see the Son of man coming in the clouds of heaven with power and great glory." That scripture is commonly presented as absolute proof for a post-tribulation rapture. That would be the case, however, only if it refers to Christ's coming to take the church to heaven. On the other hand, if it describes Christ's second coming to rescue Israel, which indeed it does, then this scripture is not teaching a post-tribulation rapture at all.

Milestone Developments

Because God's Word is completely reliable, we can have absolute confidence that, if we correctly understand prophecy, we can know the order of last-days events. I well remember how convinced were the old-time preachers of 50 years ago that two extremely significant prophesied events related to the

Rapture were fast approaching: 1) Israel's return to her own land *in unbelief*, and her rebirth as a nation; and 2) the revival of the Roman Empire, uniting Western Europe to provide a base of power for the Antichrist.

In those days, there was nothing on the world scene to give anyone hope that either of these amazing prophecies might be true. Yet the first came to pass in 1948, setting the stage for further prophesied developments. And it would now appear, after the recent break-up of the Soviet empire and the step-by-step joining of her former satellites to the growing European Union, that the second of these prophecies is well on its way to fulfillment in our day.

Israel's Rebirth

Nothing conceivable by human imagination could exceed the miracle of Israel's astonishing rebirth after centuries of desolation, the worldwide scattering of the Jews, and Hitler's Holocaust. In the nearly 60 years since then, we have seen that nation's remarkable preservation in the face of repeated military attempts to destroy her by enemies that outnumber her forty to one, and overwhelming opposition at the United Nations.

Israel is the only democracy in the Middle East and has been a member of the UN for more than 50 years. Yet it is the only one of the nearly 200-member nations that is denied the right to take its rotating term on the UN Security Council. Nearly

ARE WE THERE YET?

3,500 years ago, the Bible declared that Israel "shall not be reckoned among the nations" (Numbers 23:9).

There was even a November 1975 UN resolution that equated Zionism (the belief that Jews have the right to live in their own homeland) with racism. In effect, that resolution (reversed in 1991, over the protests of the Arab bloc) condemned the very existence of Israel—yet she will not be intimidated or die. She remains today one of the most phenomenal miracles in human history, in spite of suffering official condemnation by the UN *hundreds* of times with scarcely a whisper against those who have repeatedly attacked with the intent to annihilate her!

Israel is by far the major topic in the Bible. How overwhelmingly this is true may be seen in the following comparisons: *grace* and *gracious* together are found 201 times; *salvation* and *saved* occur 268 times; *love*, *loved*, and *lovest* are found 420 times; *peace* is found 429 times; *Christ* and *Jesus* are found 1,538 times; *Israel* and *Jacob* are found 2,923 times.

It is not surprising, then, that Israel is the major topic of Bible prophecy. There are hundreds of promises of her full and final restoration in the "promised land" in the "last days," with the Messiah reigning over her in righteousness. It is to *Israel* that Christ returns to conquer the Antichrist, to establish His kingdom, and to rule the world from Jerusalem. Nor have any been lost. The myth of the "ten lost tribes," if true, would prove the Bible false.

Paul referred to the twelve tribes as existing in his day and hoping for their restoration (Acts 26:7). James wrote his epistle "to the twelve tribes which are scattered abroad" (James 1:1). If the twelve tribes of Israel did not exist to be gathered to the land God gave them, there could be no second coming of Christ to rescue and rule over them. Christ's promise to His disciples that they would sit on the throne "judging the twelve tribes of Israel" (Luke 22:30) would be a lie and would prove that He was not the Savior. Likewise, God would have been proven a liar, and Satan would have achieved a stalemate in his battle with God for control of the universe.

Who would have dreamed a century ago—or even 50 years ago—that after the Jews had returned to this insignificant piece of real estate, it would be the focus of the world's attention week after week, year after year, decade after decade? And not casual or ordinary attention, but one born of fear and uncertainty as to how to deal with this new nation in relation to its Muslim neighbors, and of how to prevent war in that area from becoming a global holocaust. Yet what has happened is exactly what the Bible prophesied:

> Behold, I will make Jerusalem a cup of trembling unto all the people round about....And in that day will I make Jerusalem a burdensome stone for all people: all that burden themselves with it shall be cut in pieces, though all the people of the earth be gathered together against it. (Zechariah 12:2,3)

And who would have been so foolish as to imagine that, after Israel's rebirth, this Lilliputian nation's armed forces would rival in power and exceed in efficiency those of the United States and Russia! Tiny Israel, occupying about one-sixth of one percent of the land in the Arab world, has been more than a match for the surrounding Arab nations, though their tanks, planes, and other armaments outnumber hers several times over. And for decades, the Arab nations were given every possible help from the Soviets against Israel, from the latest arms to technical and strategic advisors by the thousands. After Iraq took over Kuwait in August 1990 and threatened all enemies with poison gas, syndicated columnist George Will gave the following tribute to Israel's courage and military capabilities:

> ...the West should remember with gratitude recent history's single, most effective and beneficial act of arms control, Israel's 1981 bombing of Iraq's embryonic nuclear weapons program.[3]

So far, the periodic fighting that breaks out over Israel has been confined to the Middle East. Everyone knows, however, that sooner or later a battle over that controversial land will explode into Armageddon. This, too, the Bible foretold 2,500 years ago:

> I will gather all nations against Jerusalem to battle.... Then shall the LORD go forth and fight against those

> nations....And his feet shall stand in that day upon the
> mount of Olives....And the LORD shall be king over
> all the earth. (Zechariah 14:2-4,9)

Modern Israel has many faults, for which we do not excuse her and for which she will yet taste God's judgments. She is back in her land not because of her own merit but because God is fulfilling His promises to Abraham, Isaac, and Jacob, as He swore that He would in the last days. We may be certain that the God who brought her back to her land in fulfillment of His promises, though she continues to reject her Messiah, will not allow Israel to be uprooted again (Jeremiah 30-32; Ezekiel 35-39).

The importance of Israel in last-days events and of understanding the prophecies concerning her and her land cannot be overstated. Even though Christ defeated Satan at the cross and gave proof of His victory by rising from the dead, there could be no final resolution of this battle if Satan could, by destroying the Jews, prevent God's solemn promises to Israel from being fulfilled. So far, all such attempts have failed. However, the Antichrist will stage one massive final effort to effect a permanent solution to what Hitler called the "Jewish problem." Christ himself will personally return to earth at that time to save those who have "endured to the end" (Matthew 24:13).

Nothing else in all of history comes even close to the preservation of the Jews as an identifiable ethnic group—despised worldwide, hated, persecuted, killed as no other people, exactly as foretold, and then brought back to their ancient land. Modern and tiny Israel has the greatest impact of any nation upon today's world, all in fulfillment of specific prophecies. The irrefutable fulfillment of hundreds of prophecies provides conclusive proof that God exists, that the Bible is His exclusive revelation to man, and that the Jews are His chosen people, the "apple of his eye" (Deuteronomy 32:10; Zechariah 2:8).

The Revived Roman Empire

We have also witnessed in recent years the formative stages of the fulfillment of that other strategic prophecy that I heard so much about in my youth: the revival of the ancient Roman Empire prophesied for the "last days." It has been fascinating to watch the concept of a loose union of six Western European nations under the "Treaty of Rome" gradually expand to include, as of this writing, 15 member countries, with 10 more scheduled to join shortly. A new charter is being written, and the issue of whether and in what manner to give "God" any mention is being debated. The pope argues that the charter should stress that "Christianity holds a privileged position" in Europe— a meaningless statement that neither defines "Christianity" nor its supposed privileges but that could help to prepare for Antichrist.[4] Although many students of Bible prophecy have equated the European Union (EU) with the revived Roman Empire, the Caesars controlled a far wider kingdom—the world of their day.

Formation of the EU has been only the first step, and one that students of Bible prophecy long anticipated and have been watching carefully. How could the same process extend throughout the entire territory that was once under the Caesars? That was the big question, now answered at least in part. The collapse of communism in Eastern Europe, beginning in the fall of 1989, has set in motion a process that promises to unite all nations on earth, thereby establishing the one-world government over which Antichrist will reign.

Already the door has been opened to include, in a United Europe, even the former Soviet Union and her satellites—a concept that was until very recently totally unthinkable. If this occurs, the very size, as well as the economic and military power, of the European Union (EU), stretching from the Atlantic to the farthest reaches of Siberia, will force the remainder of the world to join as well. As one well-known analyst has written:

> Membership [in the EU] is already open to those European peoples who have embraced democracy and are willing to do a deal to enter. That being so, as Europe behind the Iron Curtain liberalizes, it seems right and inevitable that the EU should expand eastward....
>
> In the very long term, the European structure will be considered the prototype for something much more ambitious. Talk of world government is at least a century old and has gone nowhere. But an ever-widening

association, based on shared cultural values, is a more
promising idea.

The European cultural concept is not a conventional idea. It is a global one. We are taking the first
steps toward an ecumenical community that will ultimately spread to all corners of our planet.[5]

This secular writer had no idea that he was reporting
on the fulfillment of one of the most important and amazing
prophecies in the Bible. The "global...ecumenical community"
to which he refers is none other than the worldwide revived
Roman Empire over which Antichrist will reign.

The revival of the Roman Empire presently underway is
not merely the latest in the long string of prophecies fulfilled
down through the centuries that demonstrate that the Bible
is, as it claims, the Word of God. More than that, it is a most
important sign of the nearness of the revelation of Antichrist
and of Christ's second coming, when He will confront the
impostor face to face here upon Planet Earth. And the Rapture
comes first!

By God's grace, I have lived long enough to see much of
what I learned in my youth as *prophecy* becoming *history*. It is
awesome to watch events unfold in consummation of prophecies recorded in the Bible thousands of years ago. The most
incredible events are yet to come, and the Bible has laid out
the script for us in advance.

How near to the end of time are we living today? Is it even possible to tell? Unfortunately, there have always been enthusiasts who were convinced that they knew exactly when the end would come, and who were able to persuade a multitude of followers to sell or give away their possessions and perch in trees or stand on hilltops to await the Second Coming. Apocalyptic theories flourish at the turn of every century, and especially at the end of a millennium, as they did again toward the end of the 1990s. Y2K alarmists (most of whom never apologized) made fortunes, while costing their followers millions—losses from which many, including trusting Christians, may never recover.

The simple fact that Antichrist must have computers to control the world should have been enough to prevent any Bible-literate Christian from being caught up in Y2K's mass hysteria. How could a global computer crash lead to a cashless society when such a society obviously needs computers to exist? How could an international banking collapse create the thriving business conditions that Christ foretold for the time of His "glorious appearing" (Titus 2:13) to His bride (Matthew 24:36-44; Luke 17:22-37)? Asking such questions will keep us from falling prey to the new hysterics that appear from time to time. Our focus must be upon our Lord and His Word.

Israel

What are prophets
  deceptive prophets exist

Scripture
  all the word of God
  all the word of man

One world global control
  stock markets, banks,
  corporations,
  principalities, governments

Knowing this first, that there shall come in the last days scoffers, walking after their own lusts, And saying, Where is the promise of his coming? for since the fathers fell asleep, all things continue as they were from the beginning of the creation.

—2 PETER 3:3–4

< 4 >

Measuring What Cannot Be Measured

Skeptics argue that the early Christians and even the Apostles, as well as countless others down through the centuries, all thought they were living in the last days, and that the term is therefore meaningless. It is true that in his sermon on the Day of Pentecost (Acts 2:17), Peter seemed to apply an Old Testament prophecy about the "last days" (Joel 2:28-32) to the outpouring of the Spirit at that time upon the disciples. However, carefully reading the context in Joel, along with Peter's words, makes it clear that Peter was not declaring that what was happening at that

< 43 >

moment was the fulfillment of Joel's promise. Rather, it was a sample of what could have occurred if Israel had repented of her rejection of Christ: She could have experienced the millennial reign of her Messiah, which Joel went on to describe. It was an offer that Israel refused (as it had been prophesied she would) but one that she will accept at a future time, after God's judgment has been fully visited upon her.

The apostle John, writing in about A.D. 95, declared: "Little children, it is the last time: and as ye have heard that antichrist shall come, even now are there many antichrists; whereby we know that it is the last time" (1 John 2:18). Yet John was by no means asserting that the "last days" had fully come, as some claim. He made it clear that although there were already many antichrists, *the Antichrist* was to appear at a future time.

Let us be reminded that the *Rapture* could have occurred at any moment. Indeed, then as now, the early church watched and waited in eager anticipation of being taken to heaven in that glorious event. There are no explicit signs to indicate that the Rapture is about to occur. The "last-days signs" are not for the *church* but for an unbelieving *Israel;* not for the Rapture but for the Second Coming. Nothing stands between the church and that "blessed hope" (Titus 2:13) of being caught up to meet her Bridegroom in the air.

Those events that Christ prophesied when He was asked for signs of His coming are intended to warn *Israel* of Antichrist's appearance and that, after guaranteeing her peace, he will seek to destroy her. Those specific signs also herald the coming of Israel's Messiah to rescue her from Antichrist's attacking armies, an event that Christians refer to as Christ's Second Coming in power and glory. Since the Rapture comes first, however, certain signs that indicate the nearness of the Second Coming may cast their shadows far enough in advance to tell the church that the Rapture must be soon. Nevertheless, we are always, regardless of any signs, to expect the Rapture to occur at any moment and to live in that expectancy (Matthew 24:44; Luke 12:35,36; Philippians 3:20; 1 Thessalonians 1:9,10; Titus 2:13; Hebrews 9:28; 1 John 3:3; Revelation 22:17,20).

As for the Second Coming, it would have been premature for Israel to expect it when only a few of the signs were yet in evidence. Jesus declared: "When ye shall see *all* these things, know that it [the Second Coming] is near, even at the doors" (Matthew 24:33). Israel has been alerted so that she might know exactly when the moment of her Messiah's intervention to save her has come. How many of these signs will cast their shadows before them at the time of the Rapture, no one can say. We do know, however, that our generation is the first for which *any* of these shadows have appeared, and we now have *many*.

The New Testament writers seem to have understood the "last days" as a time that began with the ascension of Christ and would culminate with His second coming. That event would be preceded by specific signs indicating that the generation that would exist on earth at that time would be living in the *last* of the "last days." It is exciting to note that *no generation* has ever had solid biblical reason for believing that it was living in the *last* of the last days preceding the second coming of Christ—*no generation until ours.*

Why could we believe that our generation, as opposed to all previous ones, is living in the *last* of the last days? Because so many of the major signs the Bible gives to warn of the nearness of Christ's second coming could not possibly have applied in the past but have only recently become applicable. For the first time in history, all of the signs heralding the Second Coming could come together at any moment. In fact, the present generation—*unlike any generation before it*—has more than sufficient reason for believing that the Second Coming is very near.

Signs in Our Time

What are these signs that have recently become viable for the first time in history? Jesus gave a number of them. For example, in speaking of events that would precede His second coming, He warned of a time of unprecedented destruction that would be so severe that "except those days should be shortened, there should no flesh be saved..." (Matthew 24:22). Such a statement was a puzzle to past generations: How could the destruction of all life on earth be threatened through bows and arrows, swords and spears, or even the conventional weapons of World War II? Our generation, however, has developed and stockpiled arms inconceivable in the past, which actually have the potential to destroy all life on this planet. So we are the *first generation in history* for whom this particular prophecy no longer awaits some future development to make it possible. The prophesied destruction (which Christ will intervene to stop) could occur at any moment.

In the vision of the future given to him by Christ, John saw a world ruler controlling the whole earth, not only politically and militarily, but economically as well. No one would be able to buy or sell without Antichrist's mysterious "666" stamp of approval embedded in his hand or forehead to indicate loyalty to him (Revelation 13:16-18). Although past generations took this threat seriously, there was no way that all commerce and banking on earth could be controlled from a central location, but today there is. We have the computers, communications satellites, and worldwide electronic banking networks that make such control feasible. Moreover, everyone knows that it is only a matter of time until such a system will be in place and enforced.

Only public fear of infringement of privacy and individual rights stands in the way. When these objections are outweighed by the greater urgency to stop drug traffic, money laundering, counterfeiting, credit card fraud, and terrorism, the system will be put into place. The fact that only Antichrist will enforce these controls is another persuasive argument for the manner of his advent.

John also saw that the entire world would worship Satan along with the Antichrist: "And they worshipped the dragon [that old serpent...the Devil, and Satan— (Revelation 12:9)] which gave power unto the beast [Antichrist]; and they worshipped the beast" (13:4). Such a prophecy would have seemed unbelievable in previous generations but not so in our day. Hard-core Satanism has been called "the fastest-growing subculture among America's teens."[6] Satanists have their own chaplains in the U.S. Armed Forces and are protected under freedom-of-religion laws. The accelerating explosion of Satanism worldwide is a phenomenon peculiar to our time, making the thought of the world worshiping Satan far more plausible than in past generations.

The occult world of demonic power, once the terror of primitive societies, has become the darling of the modern world, now sought after as "psychic power" in the laboratories of top universities and by military intelligence around the world. Glorified in books, video games, and movies, the "magic" of wizardry is no longer just fiction but the secret ambition of millions of teenagers. Many examples could be given, but one must suffice: *Harry Potter* books, movies, games, and toys, which are captivating millions, young and old, with the occult. More than half of the children between the ages of 6 and 17 in the U.S. have read these books, and an even higher percentage have seen the movies.

The world has experienced nothing like the Harry Potter phenomenon! In England and America, nearly 8 million copies (from the 13-million pre-release printing) of the fifth book, *Harry Potter and the Order of the Phoenix*, were sold in the first 24 hours. Imagine people waiting in line by the thousands to grab it from the shelves as stores began sales at one second after midnight June 21!

Harry is a wicked boy, disobedient to and disrespectful of parents, rebellious and disdainful of authority, mean and selfish, who uses his "magic" powers impishly—yet he is the hero and model of millions! Incredibly, as children thrill to the corrupting example of their "hero," some of today's most influential evangelical leaders see "nothing wrong" with the Harry Potter fascination sweeping Christian families. One is reminded of the prophetic words: "Woe unto them that call evil good, and good evil; that put darkness for light, and light for darkness..." (Isaiah 5:20).

Seducing Spirits, Doctrines of Devils

In a *Life* magazine interview of leading Americans on the purpose of life, the first person quoted proposed, "Our purpose is to...return to Eden, make friends with the snake [Satan] and set up our computers among the wild apple trees."[7] Such a statement in a leading magazine would have been unthinkable only a generation ago. The logo of one peace organization,

Peace On Earth, shows the world with a huge dragon (one biblical identity of Satan) perched on top and guarding it. A brochure declares what previous generations would have found shocking, but which has recently become acceptable:

> ...as we enter what has been described as the Aquarian Age, we are entering a time of cooperation between the spiritual and the material realms, so it is time for us to make peace with the dragon and work in partnership with the wisdom and the power of the earth that the dragon represents.[8]

At the same time that the world is being set up to worship the Antichrist, so is the professing Christian church. Paul's warnings are many concerning apostasy, which represents a turning away from the faith in the last days. One of the specifics he mentions seems unbelievable: "The Spirit speaketh expressly, that in the latter times some shall depart from the faith [apostatize], giving heed to seducing spirits and doctrines of devils" (1 Timothy 4:1). Such a prophecy is shocking: that a characteristic of the last days will be trafficking with evil spirits by those who call or have called themselves Christians! Yet our generation is experiencing this to a degree never before known in history.

From the pagan rulers of Egypt and Babylon to Queen Victoria and Abraham Lincoln and on into our own day, there have always been attempts by top political leaders to contact the spirit world through séances and assorted "spiritual advisors." Of course, there has also always been a fringe of society that periodically experimented with divination devices such as Ouija boards, or consulted fortune tellers, tarot cards, astrologers, etc. But with the influence of the New Age movement over the past 30 years, occultism has spread like a plague. Millions of average citizens, young and old, have been drawn into what the Bible condemns as necromancy (Leviticus 19:31; 20:6; Deuteronomy 18:9-12, etc.). Demons posing as "higher beings" are speaking through "channelers" on TV. Deluded multitudes are in daily contact with their own "inner guides" introduced to them in public schools at a young age, or later by psychologists (Carl Jung had his own "spirit guide," *Philemon*, through whom he received inspirations that still influence Christian psychologists to this day). Medical doctors, educators, and motivational speakers introduce thousands of others to "inner guides" through visualization techniques. Never before have so many been deceived into "giving heed to seducing spirits and doctrines of devils"!

Creating Antichrist's False Church

In the church, too, there is a departure from the faith— but in the *name* of faith. Seducing spirits are being contacted, but here they don't pose as "deeper levels of the psyche" or as "ascended masters" but as *Christ himself*! The practice of visualizing "Jesus" (visualizing "Mary" works just as well for Catholics) is being used in "inner healing" and in order to enhance one's prayer life or to gain a deeper insight into what Jesus taught. That the "Jesus" who appears and takes on a life of its own is not the Lord Jesus Christ but a "seducing spirit" bringing "doctrines of devils" has again been thoroughly documented in books such as *The Seduction of Christianity, Beyond Seduction,* and *Occult Invasion*, and will not be dealt with here. The *explosion* of this phenomenon, however, so that it is becoming rampant even in the church, is unique to our generation and provides further evidence that we could be in the *last* of the last days.

Paul was given remarkable insights so uniquely applicable to our modern world that they could not possibly have come to him by any means except divine inspiration. He warned, "... in the last days perilous times shall come. For men shall be lovers of their own selves" (2 Timothy 3:1,2). Mankind has always been self-centered, selfish, and narcissistic. Our generation, however, is the first one in history being *taught* to love self. It is now widely accepted that we naturally dislike ourselves and must *learn* to love ourselves before we can love God or other people. The first commandment has become "Thou shalt love thyself," relegating "Thou shalt love the Lord thy God" to second place.

Christ would never have said, "Do unto others as you would have them do unto you," if we all disliked ourselves.

His command to "love your neighbor as yourself" obviously assumes that we already love ourselves and is not intended to encourage but to *correct* self-love. It urges us to give to our neighbors some of the loving care we naturally lavish upon ourselves. Yet a popular "gospel singer," who began her career with "Guide Us, O Thou Great Jehovah," now croons, "Loving yourself is the greatest love of all." Even evangelical churches hold seminars teaching members how to love themselves. It is like pouring gasoline on a fire already out of control. And once again, the phenomenon has appeared for the first time in our present generation.

John saw in his vision that not only the dragon (Satan) would be worshiped but also that the Antichrist himself would be worshiped as God. Past generations would have thought it ridiculous to imagine that anyone, much less the entire world, would worship a *man as God*. In the last 30 years, however, the "god-men" from the East, such as Bhagwan Shri Rajneesh, Baba Muktananda, Maharaji, and many others, have come to the West and have been literally worshiped as God by thousands of their followers. Though only a small minority of mankind currently follow the gurus, nevertheless, worshiping a man as God has, for the first time in history, become commonplace in the Western world. Actors, actresses, sports heroes, and political leaders are among those now worshiping mere men posing as little gods.

When people like Shirley Maclaine, for example, claim to

be God, they are taken seriously by millions. Not long ago, they would have been classified as insane and locked up. Shirley channels her own "higher self" for guidance. Her website, www.shirleymaclaine.com, is a primer on "doctrines of devils."

In the 1960s, a young Hindu yogi of Indian ancestry, but born in Trinidad of "highly evolved" parents, accepted Christ. The young man's father, also an extremely well-respected yogi, had already withdrawn so completely from the "world of the flesh" that he never looked at, smiled at, or spoke a single word to his son. Needless to say, the young man's life changed completely when he turned his back on Hinduism. Eventually, he helped establish a Christian outreach organization in Switzerland, where he wrote the following words, already appallingly true by the late 1970s:

> I [have] observed with deep concern the rapid acceleration of a powerful but largely unrecognized Eastern influence upon the average Western mind. This invasion by Eastern religions has subtly but heavily influenced almost every area of Western society. Through the deliberate efforts of Hindu and Buddhist gurus such as Vivekananda, Aurobindo, Shri Chinmoy (who leads meditations at the United Nations in New York), and the very influential Dalai Lama, significant changes in Western thinking, beliefs, and lifestyles have been effected.

Literally millions of people have accepted Eastern presuppositions, including karma, reincarnation, and vegetarianism for religious reasons; and…millions more…have become personally involved in countless Hindu-Buddhist sects such as the Hare Krishna movement, the Self-Realization Fellowship of Yogananda, Divine Light Mission, Nichiren Shoshu, and numerous related Mind Dynamics groups, such as Silva Method….

As a former Hindu who began to travel widely throughout the West, I was astonished to observe that not only Rosicrucianism and Freemasonry have Hindu/Buddhist roots, but that almost every one of the established and respected Western sects, such as Christian Science, Science of Mind, Religious Science, and Unity is a syncretistic blend of Hinduism and Christian heresy. Even the American-born Mormon Church…is founded upon basic Hindu concepts, such as the belief in the pre-existence of the soul, a multiplicity of gods, and the teaching that godhood is the ultimate goal for humanity.[9]

The world of our day is unquestionably being prepared for the one who "as God sitteth in the temple of God, showing himself that he is God" (2 Thessalonians 2:4). This prophecy will have its primary fulfillment when the Antichrist sits in the Jewish temple yet to be rebuilt in Jerusalem. There is, however, a secondary application. The body of a believer becomes the "temple" of God through the indwelling of the Holy Spirit ("ye are the temple of God, and...the Spirit of God dwelleth in you" (1 Corinthians 3:16; cf. 6:19) and so it should be with all mankind. Instead, the religion of the Antichrist exalts *self* as "God" within the human "temple."

Today, for the first time in history, not only a few yogis and gurus but increasing millions of ordinary people worldwide are mystically looking deep within themselves. There, in what ought to be the temple of the true God, they seek to discover that their alleged "higher self" is "God." The practice of TM, Eastern meditation, and other forms of yoga is widespread. The goal is "self-realization": to realize that one is "God." It is the very same lie with which the serpent deceived Eve. Obviously the deification of self plays an important part in preparing the world to worship the Antichrist, giving us yet another indication that our generation could be living in the last of the last days.

One need not practice Eastern mysticism, however, to deify self. That philosophy is basic to humanistic psychology, which has gained prominence within the last 30 years. One of its leaders, Carl Rogers, renounced Christianity while in seminary and turned to the study of psychology. Rogers offered students a substitute secular "born again" experience of being "baptized in the fluid waters of your own self." Declaring that "self in its unlimited potential is virtually a god," Rogers defiantly demanded, "Who needs a God above when there is one within?"

Growing Religious Deception

Jesus warned that the major sign heralding the nearness of His return would be *religious deception*: "Take heed that no man *deceive* you." He clearly identified the basic elements that would characterize the prevalent last-days delusion: "Many false prophets shall rise, and shall deceive many....For there shall arise false Christs, and false prophets, and shall show great signs and wonders; insomuch that, if it were possible, they shall deceive the very elect" (Matthew 24:4,11,24).

That the Bible clearly foretold a major "signs and wonders" movement in the church in the last days is a remarkable prophecy that has been fulfilled in our time. The claim of a supposed last days revival of miracles is a major thrust of much Christian radio and television—for example, Pat Robertson's *700 Club* and the Crouch's Trinity Broadcasting Network. This claim is the major emphasis of entire ministries: Kenneth Copeland, Creflo Dollar, Kenneth Hagin, Marilyn Hickey, Benny Hinn, Joyce Meyers, Frederick Price, Oral Roberts, and a host of others. Nor can it be denied that the Bible clearly states that this movement would be deceptive and destructive.

Christ declares that He will rebuke and send away into eternal punishment many who will have claimed to have worked miracles in His name and who apparently will be those who "crept in unawares" (Jude 4): "Many will say to me in that day, Lord, Lord, have we not prophesied in thy name?

And in thy name have cast out devils? And in thy name done many wonderful works? And then will I profess unto them, I never knew you: depart from me, ye that work iniquity" (Matthew 7:22, 23).

Why will Christ reject them? Instead of faith in Christ as their claim for entrance into heaven, they profess supposed signs and wonders performed in His name—exactly what we see in many today. John Wimber, deceased leader of the Vineyard Christian Fellowship movement, even claimed in his book, *Power Evangelism*, that the gospel was virtually powerless without signs and wonders accompanying it.

Inspired of the Holy Spirit, Paul echoed Christ's warning: "Now as Jannes and Jambres withstood Moses, so do these also resist the truth: men of corrupt minds, reprobate concerning the faith" (2 Timothy 3:8). Jannes and Jambres were the magicians in Pharaoh's court who withstood Moses. How? Not by denying the miracles God did through Moses but by *duplicating* them through the power of Satan! Paul is explaining in clear terms that the greatest and most effective opposition to God's truth in the last days will not come from mocking university professors, evolutionists, and other atheists, but from professing Christians who will use "signs and wonders" performed by Satanic power to deceive many within the church—and thereby to attract success-seeking unbelievers into the growing false church left behind that will embrace Antichrist after the Rapture.

A secular analyst writing only a generation ago would not have predicted the worldwide religious revival that Christ prophesied. Instead, he would have suggested that our day would be characterized by skepticism and atheism, and that science would have advanced so far that there would be little place for religion in the world; no educated person would give credence to "spiritual values," and materialism would have taken over completely.

How wrong such an analyst would have been! In contrast, how right Christ was in saying that *many* false prophets and false messiahs would arise and deceive *many*. The implication was clear: A revival of "religion" and "spirituality" would sweep the world in the last days. It would not, however, represent the truth; instead, multitudes would be deceived by false prophets and false messiahs. The accuracy of this remarkable 2,000-year-old prophecy cannot be denied.

A Lesson from the Past

The situation in the church today is reminiscent of the last days of Israel's kingdom. Instead of heeding God's Word, God's people consulted spirit mediums (Isaiah 8:19). Israel had sunk into the mire of occultism, astrology, and idolatry (Jeremiah 19:4,5,13; 32:29). Immorality was rampant even among the priests (Ezekiel 16:15-59; Hosea 6:9). God's righteous judgment was about to fall, as it is upon today's church and world.

Nebuchadnezzar's army would be the instrument, and the long Babylonian captivity for God's chosen people would begin.

Israel desperately needed rescue from a merciless, invincible invading army, but deliverance could come only through repentance and submission to her Lord. Patiently, God had sent prophet after prophet to indict Israel for her rebellion, idolatry, wickedness, and occult practices and to plead with her to repent, but she would not. She needed to face the truth but turned instead to the numerous false prophets who lulled her to sleep with their soothing lies. Their "positive" message was far more appealing than the "negative" pronouncements of those who spoke for God. In the face of misleading assurances that all was well, Isaiah gave solemn notice: "There is no peace, saith my God, to the wicked" (Isaiah 57:21).

Earnestly Jeremiah warned of God's impending judgment against the positive-thinking false prophets who promised Israel "Peace, peace; when there is no peace" (Jeremiah 6:14; 8:11). Calling such deceitful assurances "vain vision" and "flattering divination" (Ezekiel 12:24), Ezekiel declared:

> Therefore thus saith the Lord GOD; Because ye have spoken vanity, and seen lies...I am against you....Mine hand shall be upon the prophets that see vanity, and that divine lies....Because...they have seduced my people, saying, Peace; and there was no peace.... (Ezekiel 13:8-10)

We live in a similar twilight of history, this time settling over the entire world. Once again, those who warn of God's soon-coming judgment are accused of being negative. The cure-all magic of a Positive Mental Attitude (PMA) is widely taught in the secular world of business, psychology, education, medicine—and also honored in the church.

One of the most influential churchmen of the past 50 years, praised by Billy Graham and other evangelical leaders, persuaded multitudes of professing Christians to believe:

> The world you live in is mental and not physical. Change your thought and you change everything....Your unconscious mind...[has] a power that turns wishes into realities when the wishes are strong enough....[10]
>
> Who is God? Some theological being...? God is energy. As you breathe God in, as you visualize His energy, you will be reenergized...![11]
>
> Just as there exist scientific techniques for the release of atomic energy, so are there scientific procedures for the release of spiritual energy through the mechanism of prayer...experiment with prayer power....[12]

His chief disciple, echoing his mentor, declared:

> Possibility thinking makes miracles happen.... The greatest power in the world is the power of possibility thinking.[13]

What happened to the will of God? Promoting the same occult delusion in the name of Christ, one of the most popular TV evangelists wrote a book

> ...to teach some of the basic principles that enable you to...experience the flow of God's energy...to enter the world of miracles....You can perform miracles if you but understand the...basic principles that enable you to... experience the flow of God's energy....[14]

He declared:

> I began to realize...the Bible is not an impractical book of theology, but rather a practical book of life containing a system of thought and conduct that will guarantee success [with] principles so universal they might better be considered as laws...such people as Napoleon Hill, who wrote *Think and Grow Rich*, have gleaned only a few of the truths of the kingdom of God....Some of the metaphysical principles of the kingdom, taken by themselves, can produce fantastic temporal benefits....[15]

Napoleon Hill was an occultist who learned his "metaphysical principles" from demons who came to him from the spirit world posing as masters of a "temple of wisdom."

Peale, Schuller, Robertson, Hagin, Copeland, and others, have brought into the church ancient occultism as part of the "signs and wonders" and "prosperity" movement foretold for the last days. That they are accepted so widely by Christians and praised by so many church leaders is another sign that we are in the last of the "last days" foretold in Scripture.

Many Christians now assume that our thoughts and words, not God, control our destiny—that we are little gods capable under Him of creating our own world.[16] One seminar by a well-known Christian success/motivational speaker promises, "How To Get What You Want."[17] A popular booklet by another Christian leader is titled, "How To Write Your Own Ticket With God."[18] Such a philosophy seems at obvious odds with Christ's prayer in the Garden of Gethsemane:

> Father, all things are possible unto thee; take away this
> cup [of the cross] from me: nevertheless not what I will,
> but what thou wilt. (Mark 14:36)

A Man for All Reasons

Presumably, if Christ had only understood and practiced the "principles of success" now being taught in the church, the New Testament would have had a different story to tell. Had He only taken a Dale Carnegie course in "How to Win Friends and Influence People," Jesus could have won the rabbis and Romans over to His side and wouldn't have been crucified. Instead of making enemies by His negative pronouncements, His goals could all have been worked out peacefully by the principles of Positive Thinking. But then, of course, there would be no salvation—nor could the manmade "paradise" fullfill its promises.

If a witch doctor came dancing down the aisle with his paint, feathers, fetishes, and rattles, most evangelical churches would have enough discernment to attempt to convert him—and if that didn't happen, to put him out. But the same witch doctor, minus the outward adornments of his occultism, dressed in a clerical collar or business suit, with a Ph.D. in psychology and teaching "success principles" allegedly from the Bible, would be welcomed and listened to intently.

Anthropologist Michael Harner, one of the world's leading authorities on shamanism (a modern word for witchcraft), lists the new names under which the basic elements of ancient witchcraft are now widely accepted in today's world and church: visualization, hypnosis, psychological counseling, Positive Thinking, Positive Speaking (Confession), and Eastern meditation techniques.[19] These methodologies form the foundation of New Age thinking and success techniques rampant in the business world and embraced within the church. We are seeing Satan's preparation for the ultimate delusion fulfilled in our day before our very eyes!

While guaranteed by today's "prophets" that we are in the "greatest revival ever," the church is sinking deeper into the last-days apostasy foretold by Christ and His apostles. The church has long been invaded by worldliness. Now the world has entered in a new form: New Age "spirituality." More than 40 years ago, A. W. Tozer preached that, rather than "revival," the church desperately needed *reformation*. Conditions are now far worse, making his prophetic warning even more apropos today:

> It is my considered opinion that under the present cir-
> cumstances we do not want revival at all. A widespread
> revival of the kind of Christianity we know today in
> America might prove to be a moral tragedy from which
> we would not recover in a hundred years.[20]

Yet the prospects of a humanistic world peace grow ever brighter. In spite of ethnic conflicts, Islam's continuing slaughter of non-Muslims in Israel, Sudan, Indonesia, Nigeria, the Philippines, and elsewhere, the ever-present danger of war in the Middle East, and worldwide terrorism, man is still determined to solve his problems without God and is convinced that he can do so. "Peace and safety" is the swelling cry. It is the greatest of delusions, the deceptive calm before the storm. Mankind is about to reap the full wrath of God for its rejection of His Son, who Himself is poised to return in vengeance. Surely the signs that herald the Second Coming are already casting their shadows to signal that our generation is living in the *last* of the last days.

When each of the events that we have considered stands alone, its value as a "last-days sign" may not seem too impressive. But when we see the convergence of all these events within the same time frame—and particularly the swiftness of recent developments in Eastern Europe and internationally as well—pieces of the puzzle begin to fit together.

The door seems to be opening to a *global* unification of nations and thus *global peace.* If the entire world is united, then we may be certain that the Antichrist will not rule over only a small part of it. So we move another step closer to understanding that the only sensible interpretation is a literal one of John's declaration concerning the Antichrist:

> ...and power was given him over all kindreds, and tongues, and nations. And all that dwell upon the earth shall worship him, whose names are not written in the book of life of the Lamb slain from the foundation of the world. (Revelation 13:7,8)

According to the Bible, the Antichrist will exercise his power ruthlessly, destroying three nations (Daniel 7:8), devouring and breaking in pieces (7:19). It certainly won't be a worldwide "rainbow gathering." Yet his kingdom will also have the elements of a voluntary association and democracy at first, and he will be worshiped, which certainly indicates some affection and trust. The exact picture remains a mystery.

Nuclear / War and Pestilence.
Community over privacy
Occultism and mysticism
God Man worshipped
Great wonders and miracles
Man has all the answers in humanism
One world government by Satan

7 Signs.

And without controversy great is the mystery of godliness: God was manifest in the flesh, justified in the Spirit, seen of angels, preached unto the Gentiles, believed on in the world, received up into glory.

—1 Timothy 3:16

< 5 >

Infinite Mystery, Perpetual Joy

IN A FEW MORE PAGES we will bring this book to a close by considering the majestic hope that true followers of Christ can have in the face of all the troubling attitudes, apostasies, and events we've described in the previous chapters. Hope is the antidote to all that, yet hope without a reason is no more powerful than a random belief. Nonetheless, through the grace of God, when we become familiar with the foundations of the faith that God invites us to anchor in Him, the hope we have in Christ takes wings—eventually of a literal kind! But before we talk about Hope it might be well to speak of Cause.

< 69 >

Of Jesus, John said, "In him was life; and the life was the light of men" (John 1:4). Christ declared, "I am the light of the world: he that followeth me shall not walk in darkness, but shall have the light of life" (John 8:12). The reference is not to physical light but to the spiritual light of truth—another abstract concept without any relationship to the physical universe.

"Truth" takes us beyond animal life; it has no meaning for animals. Their "intelligence" knows nothing of love, morals, compassion, mercy, or understanding but is confined to instinct and conditioned responses to stimuli. B. F. Skinner, commonly considered the founder of the Behaviorist school of modern psychology, tried to fit man into the same mold. But our ability to form conceptual ideas and express them in speech cannot be explained in terms of stimulus/response reactions. There is an impassable chasm between man and animals.

Intelligence is nonphysical because it conceives of and uses nonphysical constructs, which clearly do not originate with the material of the brain or body. This takes us beyond the physical universe into the realm of spirit. We do not know what a soul or a spirit is, or what it means that God "is a Spirit" (John 4:24) who "created man in his image" (Genesis 1:27).

God has given us sufficient proof in what we *can* verify to cause us to trust completely whatever His Word declares concerning things we cannot fully comprehend. That is where faith enters. There is much that, although we cannot understand it, we know is true. This is the case, for example, with the fact that

God is without beginning or end. It boggles our minds, but we know it must be. Unfortunately, while seeking to unravel the secrets of the universe, science neglects its Creator. The universe can lead man only to a dead end, since ultimate knowledge is hidden in the God who brought all into existence.

Though not idol worshipers in the primitive sense, scientists, university professors, business executives, and political leaders—no matter how brilliant—who do not know Christ fit the description in Romans 1 of those who reject the witness of the universe and worship the creation instead of the Creator. It is possible for Christians also to be caught up in this same materialistic emphasis and to miss *what God offers us in Himself.*

Paul's earnest desire was that all believers might attain unto "the full assurance of understanding, to the acknowledgement of the mystery of God, and of the Father, and of Christ; in whom are hid all the treasures of wisdom and knowledge" (Colossians 2:2,3).

Our knowledge of both the physical and spiritual is limited at best. But one day we will fully know when we are with Christ in our glorified bodies: "For now we see through a glass, darkly; but then face to face: now I know in part; but then shall I know even as also I am known" (1 Corinthians 13:12). When in His presence we wholly know Christ as He truly is, all limitations will have vanished, even our lack of power to fully overcome sin: when we see Him, "we shall be like him, for we shall see him as he is" (1 John 3:2). Knowing Christ is everything!

A God of Infinite Majesty

The concept of one true God who exists eternally in three Persons (Father, Son, and Holy Spirit) is rejected even by some who claim to be Christians. Yet this is taught all through Scripture, in the Old Testament as well as in the New. Consider: "I have not spoken in secret from the beginning; from the time that it was, there am I...." Surely the speaker who has been in existence forever must be God himself. Yet He declares, "the Lord God, and his Spirit, hath sent me" (Isaiah 48:16). Here we have the eternal love of God, who is the Word, declaring that the Father and Holy Spirit sent Him on a mission to this earth. We cannot comprehend the mystery of the Trinity; yet that is no more reason to doubt it than to doubt anything else that we know is real but cannot comprehend.

If God were a single being (as Muslims believe Allah to be and most Jews believe Yahweh is), He would have had to create creatures in order to experience love, fellowship, and communion. The biblical God *is* love in Himself, manifesting plurality in the Godhead: "The Father loveth the Son..." (John 5:20). God must be one; but He must comprise both singularity and plurality.

Only God could pay the infinite penalty His justice demands for sin. But that would not be just, because "God is not a man..." (Numbers 23:19). The incarnation is therefore essential—but impossible if God were a singular being. "The Father sent the Son to be the Saviour of the world" (1 John 4:14). It was Jesus who died on the cross, not the Father nor the Holy Spirit.

Neither could a mere man, being finite, pay that infinite penalty. All through the Old Testament, Yahweh declares that He is the only Savior (Isaiah 43:3,11; 45:15,21; 49:26; Hosea 13:4, etc.). Thus Jesus had to be Yahweh but also a man. When God the Son became a man, He did not and could not cease to be God. Jesus was both God and man.

How could God become a man? Again, that is only possible through the Trinity. The Father didn't become man, nor did the Holy Spirit. Even though we cannot understand this, we know it must be so. The penalty for our sins is infinite because God and His justice are infinite. Consequently, those who reject Christ's payment on their behalf will be separated from God forever.

How evil could arise in God's "good" universe (Genesis 1:31) is a mystery—"the mystery of iniquity" (2 Thessalonians 2:7). It will reach its fullness in Antichrist, through whom Satan will rule the world. In Antichrist, as God was manifested in Christ, so Satan will be manifested in the flesh, although not in the "fullness of the Godhead" of Christ (Colossians 2:9).

Satan must be brilliant beyond our comprehension, apparently second only to God in power and understanding. It is a mystery that Satan, having known intimately the holy and glorious presence and power of God on His throne, could ever have dared, much less desired, to rebel. How could he have imagined that he could ever defeat God? Surely, this is a great mystery!

Satan was not raised in a "dysfunctional family" or in a ghetto, nor was he "abused as a child." None of the standard excuses for rebellious and selfish behavior accepted by today's Christian psychologists applies to Satan—or to Adam and Eve. To accept any explanation for evil that doesn't fit them is to be deceived. Certainly today's popular diagnosis of "low self-esteem" or a "poor self-image" was not Satan's problem!

Scripture says he was lifted up with pride: "O covering cherub....Thine heart was lifted up because of thy beauty" (Ezekiel 28:17). He is apparently a self-deceived ego-maniac, blinded by pride in his own power and abilities.

Here is the mystery of iniquity: In the very presence of God, in the heart of the cherub closest to God, the ultimate evil was conceived. By one fateful choice, the most beautiful, powerful, and intelligent angelic being became for all time the ultimate in evil: the arch enemy of God and man, the "great dragon...that old serpent, called the Devil, and Satan, which deceiveth the whole world" (Revelation 12:9; 20:2).

Paul warns that a man should not become an elder until he is mature in the faith, "Not a novice, lest being lifted up with pride he fall into the condemnation of the devil" (1 Timothy 3:6). This tells us again that pride was Satan's downfall—and is man's besetting sin as well. "Pride goeth before destruction, and an haughty spirit before a fall" (Proverbs 16:18).

It is also a mystery that Eve would believe the serpent's lie contradicting what her gracious Creator had said. Adam was not deceived (1 Timothy 2:14). No doubt out of love for Eve and not wanting to be separated from her, he joined her in disobedience, knowing the consequences. It remains a mystery, however, that *anyone* would rebel against God, that *anyone* would choose the pleasures of the moment in exchange for eternal separation from God.

The heart of this mystery is the autonomy of intelligent created beings who clearly have something called self-will. At least some angels (Satan and those who joined his rebellion) and all men have the power of choice. In deciding upon beliefs or actions, though evidence may be weighed, ultimately reason is set aside in order to bow before the throne of self. We are our own worst enemies.

Self had its awful birth when Eve made the choice of disobedience for all of her descendants. Christ said there is no hope except we deny self (Matthew 16:24). And the only way that can be done effectively is to embrace the cross of Christ as our own so that we can say with Paul, "I am crucified with Christ: nevertheless I live; yet not I, but Christ liveth in me..." (Galatians 2:20).

Solving the Problem of Evil

The solution to the problem of evil, through the incarnation, is also a mystery. "...[G]reat is the mystery of godliness: God was manifest in the flesh, justified in the Spirit, seen of angels, preached unto the Gentiles, believed on in the world, received up into glory" (1 Timothy 3:16).

"God was manifest in the flesh." What a mystery! God could become a fetus in Mary's womb? John the Baptist as a six-month-old fetus leapt in the womb of Elizabeth in recognition that Mary was pregnant with the Messiah. Amazing!

"Seen of angels." These heavenly beings must have watched in astonishment. The One whom they had known as God the Son, one with the Father, for at least 4,000 years by earth time (we know not how much earlier angels were created), was united with a human body growing in the virgin Mary's womb, soon to be born a babe needing a mother's milk and care—truly man, yet at the same time truly God. Mystery of mysteries!

"Believed on in the world." The Apostle John speaks in awe of this One whom "we have heard...seen with our eyes...looked upon, and our hands have handled, of the Word of life. (For the life was manifested, and we have seen it, and bear witness, and shew unto you that eternal life, which was with the Father, and was manifested unto us)" (1 John 1:1, 2). In his Gospel, John says, "The Word was made flesh, and dwelt among us (and we beheld his glory, the glory as of the only begotten of the Father), full of grace and truth" (John 1:14).

Yes, *"Believed on in the world."* Certainly John believed, as did Paul, that Jesus the Messiah of Israel was truly "God manifest in the flesh." To be a Christian one must believe that Jesus Christ is God, come as a man to redeem us. What love, to come from so high to stoop so low—to be rejected, hated, misunderstood, mocked, maligned, stripped, scourged, and crucified by those He came to redeem!

"Received up into glory." His sacrifice accepted by the Father, He is glorified at the "Father's right hand" and interceding there for us (Romans 8:34). But even before that great meeting in His presence in the Father's house, "beholding as in a glass the glory of the Lord, [we] are changed into the same image...by the Spirit of the Lord" (2 Corinthians 3:18).

Surely, if the incarnation is the great mystery of godliness, then for us to live godly lives we must have Christ dwelling within us and living His life through us: "Christ in you, the hope of glory, whom we preach..." (Colossians 1:27, 28). This is the "hope of his calling," which Paul prayed that the Ephesian saints would understand. Peter explains that God "hath called us unto his eternal glory" (1 Peter 5:10). We are going to be like Christ. The glory that the disciples beheld in Christ will be manifested in us!

We are transformed by His Word, the Word of Truth upon which we feed for spiritual nourishment. This is the living Word of God, which, when believed, (1 Peter 1:23-25) creates and nourishes spiritual life.

Eastern mysticism ancient!
Israel chosen, to ?!?
Not accepted - rejected
That's the mystery "
Romans 1

We love him, because he first loved us.

—1 JOHN 4:19

< 6 >

The Ultimate Hope

THE CHRISTIAN LIFE should be one of great joy for many reasons. First of all, the knowledge that one has been forgiven of every sin by God, and that no appeasement need be made, gives a joyful release from the fear of coming judgment. Then there is the deep gratitude that Christ would suffer the eternal judgment we deserved in order to have us in His presence in heaven forever. There is also the joy of love awakened by the Holy Spirit in response to His great love—a love that is beyond anything earth can offer. This love gives the believer a

< 79 >

consuming desire to please the One who said, "If ye love me, keep my commandments" (John 14:15).

Perhaps the greatest joy of all is the discovery that we can indeed please the One who loves us so—that our hearts have been changed so that we now hate sin and love righteousness. Words fail to express the joy that comes from knowing that Christ himself is living within us and empowers us by His Holy Spirit to live a new life that honors and glorifies Him. Instead of fearing to meet God, we long to be in the presence of our heavenly Father when at last, as part of the church, which is Christ's bride, we will see the Bridegroom and be united with Him forever.

To be caught up at the Rapture to meet Christ in the air and to be taken to heaven without experiencing physical death is the great hope of the Christian. By comparison, any earthly ambition fades into insignificance. Paul reminded the Philippians, "Our conversation [citizenship] is in heaven; from whence also we look for the Saviour, the Lord Jesus Christ" (3:20). To Titus he wrote: "Looking for that blessed hope, and the glorious appearing of the great God and our Saviour Jesus Christ" (2:13). Hebrews 9:28 declares, "Unto them that look for him [Christ] shall he appear the second time without sin unto salvation."

One does not look for someone who cannot possibly appear for months, much less for years. If the Rapture could not occur until after the Antichrist had first appeared, or until the end of the Great Tribulation, surely such language would

not have been used. There can be no doubt that the imminent
return of Christ to take them to His Father's house of many
mansions was the daily hope and expectancy of the early
Christians. And so it should be for us today. These words of our
Lord should both encourage and warn us:

> Let your loins be girded about, and your lights burn-
> ing; and ye yourselves like unto men that wait for their
> lord....Blessed are those servants whom the lord when
> he cometh shall find watching....Be ye therefore ready
> also: for the Son of man cometh at an hour when ye
> think not. (Luke 12:35-37,40)

"At an hour when ye think not"! That expression would
suggest that the nearer the coming of the Lord, the fewer there
will be who are really looking for Him. It seems odd that it
should be so, yet the expectancy in the church of Christ's
return has been steadily decreasing and is now at a very low
ebb. It also suggests that conditions in the world will be such
when Christ returns that Christians will be so contented and
at ease that they will not be longing to leave this earth for a
better place. Paul's warning, which we have quoted several
times, bears repeating yet again: "When they say 'Peace and
safety'…" then the big surprise will come!

There are Christians today who complain that those who
are looking for Christ to return at any moment are "so heavenly

minded that they're no earthly good." But that cliché has it backward. Jesus, who is our example, was the most heavenly minded Person in history—yet at the same time, He did the most earthly good. True "heavenly mindedness" actually makes one more useful here upon earth.

Others suggest that those who are waiting for the Rapture to take them to heaven are just sitting on their hands and doing nothing. Critics call this an "escapist mentality." Logically, however, the deeper the conviction that time is short, the more diligent we will be to do God's will, live for Christ, and win others for Him. This "blessed hope" of being with our Lord in heaven at any moment is in fact the greatest motivation of all for holy and victorious living. John said that everyone who has this hope "purifieth himself, even as he [Christ] is pure" (1 John 3:3).

The Standard and Power

In Colossians 3, Paul gives as complete a description as we can find anywhere in Scripture of the Christian life—what we should and what we should not be and do. The Christian is to mortify his bodily passions: "fornication, uncleanness, inordinate affection, evil concupiscence, and covetousness, which is idolatry...anger, wrath, malice, blasphemy, filthy communication...", and so forth. Having done that, he is to express in holiness and love "mercies, kindness, humbleness of mind, meekness, longsuffering...." The list goes on, providing a complete pattern of godliness. In that one chapter, the Apostle Paul clearly presents the Christian life in unmistakable and practical terms.

Of course, most religions have moral standards and require a code of behavior for their adherents to follow. Buddha had his Four Noble Truths and Eightfold Path, Confucius his secular ethical philosophy. Other religions have their standards that, to some extent, reflect God's moral laws written in everyone's conscience. It is axiomatic, however, that no ethical philosophy can provide the moral strength to live up to its standards. No law can save; it can only condemn. Christianity, which sets by far the highest standard of all, is alone in providing the power to live a holy life. Therein lies another element of the uniqueness that separates it from every religion the world has ever known.

Paul did not impose upon the Colossian believers, or upon us today, a strict moral code that we must struggle to live up to in our own strength. The key to living the Christian life is found in one word in verses 5 and 12: *therefore*. "Mortify *therefore*" the sins of the flesh. "Put on *therefore*" the holiness and graces of Christ. Whatever *therefore* refers to, it gives both the *reason* for obedience and the *power* to obey. To what, then, does it allude? The answer is found in the preceding verses:

> If [since] ye then be risen with Christ, seek those things
> which are above, where Christ sitteth on the right hand
> of God. Set your affection on things above, not on things
> on the earth. For ye are dead, and your life is hid with
> Christ in God. When Christ, who is our life, shall appear,
> then shall ye also appear with him in glory. Mortify
> *therefore*.... Put on *therefore*.... (Colossians 3:1-4)

The power to live the Christian life comes from confidence
in and gratitude for the marvelous, historic fact that Christ
died for our sins, rose from the dead, and is now in heaven at
the Father's right hand. Yet there is another dynamic: the great
hope of His soon appearing and of our appearing with Him
as His bride at His side! This is no mere theological religious
philosophy, but a vital, real relationship with One who could
come at any moment to take us to be forever in His presence in a new, eternal dimension of living! Once that hope
has gripped us, we have the motivation and power to live as
truly born again and as God's dear children, partakers of His
divine nature.

Moreover, true Christians have a deep sense of the holiness of God and an awesome, respectful fear of the One to
whom they must give account. They have a keen awareness
of having broken His law, and they know the awful consequences of this. That is why they are so grateful that their sins
have been forgiven. Until a person has been brought to these

convictions, he is not ready to become a Christian on the terms that God offers in the Bible.

Yes, the Christian is crucified with Christ, dead to sin and to this world, and intimately identified with Christ in His cross. He has been raised with Him into new life—in fact, Christ *is* our life. But in addition to all of this, wonderful as it is, Paul exhorts us to live in this expectancy: "When Christ, who is our life, shall appear, then shall ye also appear with him in glory." The knowledge of that destiny delivers us from lusts and fears and causes this world to lose its attractiveness to us once and for all.

Christ could come at any moment to take us to His Father's house, where we will be united with Him eternally. Then, when He appears and "every eye shall see Him" and Israel will recognize Him, we will be at His side in glorified bodies to rule and reign with Him—"and so shall we ever be with the Lord!" That is the Christian's hope. Heaven is our real home and that is where our hearts are—with Him. The world has lost its appeal, sin has lost its power, and Satan must relinquish his claim upon those who belong to Christ. We have been set free!

The Purifying Expectation

Moreover, it is essential that the imminent rapture once again become not only the great expectancy and hope of the church, but that Christians testify to the world of this soon-coming event and of Christ's second coming to judge the world and to establish His millennial kingdom that will follow. If we believe in the Christ whose birth the angels proclaimed, then we must also embrace what the angels declared to be the purpose of His birth: that He would bring peace to this earth, as only He can, by personally reigning on the throne of His father David in Jerusalem. This is not stated as an ideal possibility with other options available; it is man's *only* hope.

Those who believe in Christ must necessarily oppose and condemn as false and deceitful every attempt to bring "peace on earth" that does not embrace Jesus Christ as world ruler. If that seems like an extreme statement, it is only because so few Christians take seriously what the Bible says about global peace, the Rapture, the rise of Antichrist, and the Second Coming.

Those who set out to establish international peace through a world government over which the Lord Jesus Christ is not invited to reign are necessarily on the side of the Antichrist. They are preparing the world for his rule, whether they acknowledge that fact or not, even though the prospect for international peace and unity resulting from their own efforts may seem so encouraging.

Those who suggest that we can retain the idea of Christ's return to reign over this earth merely as the symbol of some "spiritual truth" suitable for all religions deny the very foundation of the Christian faith. The significant distinction between Christianity and every other world religion is found in the central and essential *personal* role that Christ plays as compared with that of a Buddha, Muhammad, Krishna, or Confucius. In contrast to others, Christ did not offer a mere religious philosophy to live by; He offered *Himself*.

Christ *personally* died for our sins upon the cross, and He promises to *personally* live within the hearts of those who receive Him as Savior and Lord. Furthermore, He promised just as clearly to come *personally, visibly,* and *physically* to this earth to establish His kingdom in peace and righteousness. It is as much a denial of the Christian faith to refuse to take seriously Christ's promise to return in person upon earth as it is to reject His offer to personally be one's Savior from sin and its penalty.

"Compel Them to Come In"

At least 50 million people, and perhaps many more, turned to Christ in China during the brief period of increased freedom that followed the demise of Mao Tse Tung and his totalitarian regime. Concerned by this revival, Chinese authorities had already begun to imprison and even execute Christian leaders long before the student uprising and massacre at Tiananmen Square in early June 1989—peaceful demonstrations that were led, to a large extent, by Christians. Since that time, and particularly since the fall of Communist regimes in Europe, conditions in China have grown increasingly more difficult. There is great fear on the part of the leaders that the army could rise up as it did in Romania, and measures are being taken to prevent popular demonstrations of any kind. It seems likely that a new wave of repression against religion will be launched.

The new breath of freedom in Eastern Europe could well bring a similar revival there. As this book goes to press, there are indications that multitudes are coming to Christ. The following are brief excerpts from a few representative letters from the countries that formerly made up the Soviet Union, where so many are now believing the gospel after hearing it for the first time:

> I was a member of the Communist Party for 25 years. How much harm I caused Christians! But God forgave me. I can't believe the depth of His love. (from Rovno)

> Together with some friends, I decided to rob a church.... I came to the church to case the place and heard a sermon that was just for me....I repented. My friends think I'm crazy but I am praying for them. I want to tell everyone about Jesus. (from Grodno)

> I was a hardened atheist....But now by God's will I am proving that He does exist. (from Arkhangelsk)

> I am already 80 years old and I just received my first copy of the Bible....I weep with great joy that God has sent me bread from heaven. (From Zaporozhe)[21]

There are reports of many people who, upon hearing their first sermon or getting their first copy of the Bible, are being set free from sin and self for eternity. The following letter to the editor from a young man in Novosibirsk, Siberia, was published in the popular Soviet weekly *Ogonyok*. It eloquently tells the story of what is happening to thousands:

> I just turned over the last page of a great book, and I am overcome by feelings of gratitude and happiness. But there are some bitter questions which remain unanswered: Why only now, why so late? Half of my life is gone! Oh, if it could only have been 10 years earlier!… At the age of 30 I was able to read the Gospel for the very first time.
>
> It was entirely by chance that this small book fell into my hands…and I was gripped by what I read…. But gradually I began to boil with indignation: To think that such a treasure had been hidden from me! Who decided and on what grounds that this book was harmful to me? I realized that I have never been and never will be an atheist.
>
> In our time of unrest and brokenness, when crystal palaces turn out to be cardboard shacks, when once majestic kings are now covered with shame, when under the granite edifices are unstable foundations of clay, then I know that there is a book to which I can always return, and it will help, comfort and support me in the darkest hour.

Perfection for Eternity

That "darkest hour" is probably nearer than most of us imagine. There is an old saying that the night seems the darkest just before the dawn. The Bible, on the other hand, cautions us that things will seem the brightest for mankind just before earth's darkest hour. Unperturbed by events, whatever they may bring, the Christian's hope remains firm:

> For I reckon that the sufferings of this present time are not worthy to be compared with the glory which shall be revealed in us. (Romans 8:18)
>
> For our light affliction, which is but for a moment, worketh for us a far more exceeding and eternal weight of glory.... (2 Corinthians 4:17)
>
> If we suffer [for him], we shall also reign with him: if we deny him, he also will deny us. (2 Timothy 2:12)

To "reign with Him"! That hope is not fueled by a selfish lust for power but by love and compassion for this suffering earth and its inhabitants. The King with whom we will reign over this world in resurrected, glorified bodies is the Creator and Lord of the universe. He is also the One who loved mankind so much that He became one of us in order to die for our sins. How different His benevolent rule of perfect righteousness will be, not only from the destructive rule of Antichrist but from the best that humanistic politicians could possibly offer!

The most heroic efforts of environmentalists can only fall short of rescuing earth's ecological system from the cumulative results of human carelessness, abuse, and exploitation. In contrast, Christ will restore this earth to its pollution-free, Edenic beauty and peacefulness. In the Millennium there will no longer be any need for a Society for the Prevention of Cruelty to Animals. Nor will the creatures themselves bite and devour one another. The pitiful suffering of even a fly caught in a spider's web will be ended:

> The wolf also shall dwell with the lamb, and the leopard shall lie down with the kid; and the calf and the young lion and the fatling together; and a child shall lead them.
>
> And the cow and the bear shall feed; their young ones shall lie down together: and the lion shall eat straw like the ox.
>
> The sucking child shall play on the hole of the asp, and the weaned child shall put his hand on the cockatrice' den....[F]or the earth shall be full of the knowledge of the LORD, as the waters cover the sea. (Isaiah 11:6-8)

Poverty and famine and the crippling diseases of old age will be gone forever. Robust good health and happiness will bless all mankind. With abundance for all, there will be no cause for greed, envy, anger, and hatred. Satan's confinement and Christ's perfect reign for 1,000 years will make even the pettiest crimes rare. Earth will be a paradise of blessing and joy beyond present comprehension. The Millennium will display the beauties of the colorful, flowering, fruitful environment that God originally planned—a world of love and peace and joy in human relationships as well.

Wonderful though it will be, however, the Millennium is not the ultimate kingdom that the prophets foretold: "Of the increase of his government and peace there shall be no end..." (Isaiah 9:7). It ends after 1,000 years—tragically and violently—in war. The Millennium is, in fact, the final proof of mankind's incorrigibly sinful and selfish nature. The theories of psychologists and sociologists, which blame "society" and "environment" for mankind's ills, will be laid to rest. Just as Satan incited Eve to rebellion in the perfect Garden of Eden, so he will, when released after 1,000 years, entice the nations to attack Christ:

> And when the thousand years are expired, Satan shall be loosed out of his prison, and shall go out to deceive the nations which are in the four quarters of the earth, Gog and Magog, to gather them together to battle: the number of whom is as the sand of the sea.
>
> And they went up on the breadth of the earth, and compassed the camp of the saints about, and the beloved city: and fire came down from God out of heaven and devoured them. (Revelation 20:7-9)

God's ultimate kingdom is far more wonderful than human imagination can even conceive: "Eye hath not seen, nor ear heard, neither have entered into the heart of man, the things which God hath prepared for them that love him" (1 Corinthians 2:9). The entire universe, so contaminated and debilitated by Satan's cosmic rebellion, will vanish in one huge nuclear explosion, to be replaced instantly by a "new heavens and a new earth, wherein dwelleth righteousness" (2 Peter 3:13).

The new universe will be inhabited by those who have repented and received God's remedy so that He could create them anew (Ephesians 2:8-10). In perfect bodies, no longer susceptible to temptation and sin, and filled with Christ's love, theirs will be eternal bliss in God's presence and the inconceivable adventure and joy of the wonders He has planned for all eternity.

At any moment it could be too late to respond, but as yet, Christ's gracious offer of pardon and eternal joy is still open: "He that heareth my word, and believeth on him that sent me, hath everlasting life, and shall not come into condemnation; but is passed from death unto life" (John 5:24). "Therefore if any man be in Christ, he is a new creature: old things are passed away; behold, all things are become new!" (2 Corinthians 5:17).

Endnotes

1. William Manchester, *The Last Lion: Biography of Winston Churchill, 1932-40* (Little, Brown and Company, 1988), 82-83.

2. Benjamin Netanyahu, *Fighting Terrorism* (Noonday Press, 1997),114.

3. George Will, "Hussein worse than Mussolini in viciousness, military might" (syndicated column, Washington, D.C.).

4. "EU debates God's place in its charter,"*USA Today*, February 6, 2002, 8a.

5. Paul Johnson, "Entering the 'Age of Deals'," *World Press Review*, March 1990, 24-25.

6. *Satanism In America* (Kerusso Company, Inc., P.O. Box 1168, Crocket, TX 75835), 34, endorsed by The National Criminal Justice Task Force on Occult Related Ritualistic Crimes.

7. "The Meaning of Life," *Life* magazine, December 1988, 78.

8. Brochure of Peace on Earth, Baltimore, Maryland.

9. Rabi R. Maharaj, *Death of a Guru* (Harvest House, 1984), 178-79.

10. Norman Vincent Peale, *Positive Imaging* (Fawcett Crest, 1982), 77.

11. Norman Vincent Peale, *Plus: The Magazine of Positive Thinking*, Vol. 37, no. 4 (Part II), May 1986, 23.

12. Norman Vincent Peale, *The Power of Positive Thinking* (Fawcett Crest, 1983), 52-53.

13. Robert Schuller, *Your Church Has Real Possibilities!* (Regal Books, 1974), 85.

14. Pat Robertson with William Proctor, *Beyond Reason: How Miracles Can Change Your Life* (William Morrow and Company, Inc., 1985), 20.

15. Pat Robertson with Bob Slosser, *The Secret Kingdom: A Promise of Hope and Freedom in a World of Turmoil* (Thomas Nelson Publishers, 1982), 43-46, 69.

16. For a full discussion of this belief and those who teach it, see Dave Hunt and T. A. McMahon, *The Seduction of Christianity* (Harvest House, 1985).

17. Zig Ziglar, "How To Get What You Want" (tape No. 1105 in W. Clement Stone's "Collections of Cassette Tapes" offered by PMA, Chicago, IL and advertised in Robert Schuller's *Possibilities* magazine).

18. By Kenneth Hagin.

19. Michael J. Harner, *The Way of the Shaman: A Guide to Healing and Power* (Harper & Row, 1980), 136.

20. A. W. Tozer, *Keys to the Deeper Life* (Zondervan, 1988) rev. expanded ed., 18.

21. These paragraphs come from just a few of the thousands of letters being received in response to broadcasts into the countries that formerly made up the USSR, by Russian Christian Radio, P.O. Box 1667, Estes Park, CO 80517.

About The Berean Call

*The Berean Call (TBC) is a nonprofit,
tax-exempt corporation which exists to:*

ALERT believers in Christ to unbiblical teachings and practices impacting
the church

EXHORT believers to give greater heed to biblical discernment and truth
regarding teachings and practices being currently promoted in the
church

SUPPLY believers with teaching, information, and materials which will
encourage the love of God's truth, and assist in the development of
biblical discernment

MOBILIZE believers in Christ to action in obedience to the scriptural
command to "earnestly contend for the faith" (Jude 3)

IMPACT the church of Jesus Christ with the necessity for trusting
the Scriptures as the only rule for faith, practice, and a life pleasing
to God

*A free monthly newsletter, THE BEREAN CALL, may be received
by sending a request to: PO Box 7019, Bend, OR 97708; or by calling*

1-800-937-6638

*To register for free email updates, to access our digital archives, and to
order a variety of additional resource materials online, visit us at:*

www.thebereancall.org

BEND • OREGON

Printed in Great Britain
by Amazon